BRITAIN'S █ HERITAGE

The Sixties Railway

Greg Morse

AMBERLEY

Acknowledgements

I am indebted to Roger Badger, Bridget Eickhoff, Derek Hotchkiss, Philip Hunt, Mick James, Julia Jenkins, Gerald Riley, Debbie Stevens, Michael Woods and Nick Wright.

My thanks also go to those who supplied many of the images in this book: David Christie, Colour-Rail (incorporating the work of G. C. Bett, the G. Devine Collection, K. C. H. Fairey, Barry Gant, G. Goodall, John E. Henderson, P. J. Hughes, C. Leigh-Jones, T. B. Owen, and G. Pratt), Rail Photoprints (Hugh Ballantyne, Alan H. Bryant ARPS, Ronald F. Collen-Jones, John Chalcraft, David Cobbe, Charlie Cross, Chris Davies, the Gordon Edgar Collection, Norman Preedy, David Rostance, and Colin Whitfield), Getty Images, Colin J. Marsden and STEAM Museum, Swindon.

About the Author

Greg Morse was instilled with a love of trains at an early age. Growing up in the Great Western town of Swindon in the 1970s, he witnessed the end of the celebrated diesel-hydraulics and the birth of the Inter-City 125s. He has written many articles and books on railway history and is now privileged to work for the industry he loves as an Operational Safety Specialist.

Cover: The Sixties Railway – and the change it underwent – is captured perfectly by this 1964 Shrewsbury scene. On the left is D1586, a virtually brand-new Brush Type 4, while on the right the ebbing tide of steam is summed up by grimy ex-Great Western No. 6944 *Fledborough Hall*.

First published 2017

Amberley Publishing
The Hill, Stroud
Gloucestershire, GL5 4EP

www.amberley-books.com

Copyright © Greg Morse, 2017

The right of Greg Morse to be identified as the Author of this work has been asserted in accordance with the Copyrights, Designs and Patents Act 1988.

ISBN 978 1 4456 6576 4 (paperback)
ISBN 978 1 4456 6577 1 (ebook)

British Library Cataloguing in Publication Data.
A catalogue record for this book is available from the British Library.

Printed in the UK.

Contents

1
Introduction: An Autumn Chill in Springtime

It was hard to see what was happening at first. So many men had wanted to be there that bittersweet spring day. A large number had worked on her, of course – forming the boiler, fitting the frame, forging the firebox, turning the pistons. Hours of effort – hours of *skill* – had made her ready: a vision in lined green, copper-capped chimney shining, a curtain veiling eleven letters of brass.

At last, you nudge your way to the front and rest your hand on the ropes. Some of the men are grumbling – it's not a proper engine, they say – not a Great Western one ... all those pipes on show ... an untidy looking thing! Better, you suggest, than the diesels taking shape in 'A' Shop. The chorus of agreement fades and the nodding heads hold still as Mr Hanks – chairman of the Western Area Board – steps up to make his speech ...

Evening Star – the last steam locomotive to be built for British Railways – is named at its birthplace, Swindon Works, on 18 March 1960.

The crowds gather to watch *Evening Star*'s naming ceremony.

> ... no other product of man's mind has ever exercised such a compelling hold upon the public's imagination as the steam locomotive. No other machine in its day has been a more faithful friend to mankind nor has contributed more to the growth of industry ...

The Commission's Keith Grand pulls the cord to reveal the name: *Evening Star*, an engine that will power the 'Pines' over the Mendips and on to Bournemouth; an engine whose number'll be noted by boys who thought their world would never end... But nothing lasts forever, and the drive for modernisation that made this the last steam locomotive to be built will see them all gone within eight years. By then, Messrs Hanks and Grand will have long lost their positions and the Mendips will have lost its trunk route. Yesterday's men, yesterday's locomotive, yesterday's line. But what of tomorrow?

* * * * * *

Evening Star was named at Swindon Works on 18 March 1960. That same month, a group of men met at the behest of Transport Minister Ernest Marples, who was seeking ways of cutting the cost of change on the railway. Headed by the chairman of Tube Investments, Sir Ivan Stedeford, the so-called Stedeford Committee would report later that year, its recommendations leading (*inter alia*) to the replacement of the British Transport Commission by a new British Railways Board. One member of that group would go on to create more change, streamlining the network by suggesting the closure of some 6,000 route miles, while bringing a new rigour to staff appraisals, staff training and staff management. Yet Doctor Richard Beeching too would be gone by 1965, as the political tide turned and the industry began to look towards an 'Inter-City' era of sleek stations, superior service and higher speeds. According to the publicity department, at least ...

In full flight: *Evening Star* takes an express over Masbury Summit on the Somerset & Dorset line in August 1962.

The last steam locomotive alongside steam's replacement. Just six years old, *Evening Star* waits at Severn Tunnel Junction for repair and eventual preservation. Alongside in this March 1966 view is an English Electric Type 3.

2

The Commission
De-Commissioned

For some it was the best of times, for others it was closer to the worst. More and more people may have been buying scooters, cars, televisions and transistor radios, but all those purchases meant a payments crisis was looming as 1960's summer turned to autumn. In Whitehall, Prime Minister Harold MacMillan was grappling with a treasury that wanted a fierce budget to curb inflation; in 222 Marylebone Road – once the Great Central Hotel, now home to the British Transport Commission – Chairman Sir Brian Robertson was growing ever more uneasy about that same department's intentions.

Formed on nationalisation, the BTC originally oversaw not only British Railways, but also bus companies, road hauliers, docks, hotels, canals, tramways, shipping lines, London Transport – even a film unit – in order to provide 'an efficient, adequate, economical and properly integrated system of public inland transport and port facilities within Great Britain for passengers and goods'. Alas, that valiant hope was never satisfied, and the loss of traffic from the mid-1950s, coupled with poor industrial relations and the rising cost of modernisation, meant it entered the new decade in a somewhat parlous state.

Like *Evening Star*, No. 70006 *Robert Burns* – seen here at Liverpool Street – was designed for BR by Robert Riddles. Soon, though, diesels like the BRCW Type 2 in the background will encroach on more and more traffic that was once the preserve of steam.

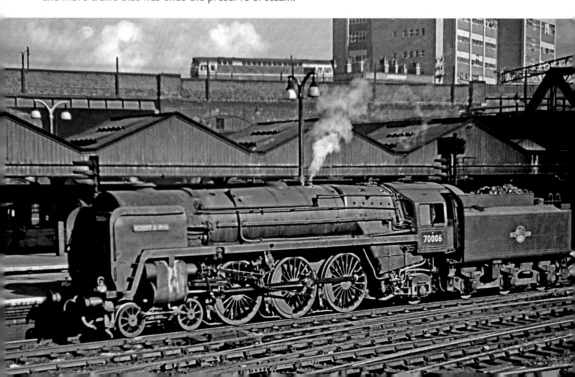

Did you know?

The Transport Act of 1947 brought the Great Western, London Midland & Scottish, London & North Eastern and Southern railways (along with fifty smaller concerns) into public ownership from 1 January 1948. Trading as 'British Railways', the network was divided into six regions (the Eastern, London Midland, North Eastern, Scottish, Southern, and Western), above which sat an executive, one of five that answered to the British Transport Commission. This structure lasted until 1953, when abolition of the Railway Executive allowed direct contact between the BTC and the regions.

The government was not blameless in this, its Transport Act of 1953, while reducing some of the Commission's over-bureaucratic structure, also sold off the road-haulage industry, creating a phalanx of private firms, whose prices beat BR's on almost every level. An increasing number of freight customers took advantage of the competition but, though technology seemed to offer a solution, it built a new world that was at once brave and Byzantine.

The *Modernisation and Re-Equipment of British Railways* – the 'Modernisation Plan', published at the very end of 1954 – had been supported by the same government, which set aside £1,200 million of public money to be spent on colour-light signalling, mechanisation and permanent way improvements. Much of the fund would also smooth the substitution of steam by diesel and electric traction. For the former, a 'Pilot Scheme' was developed to test various transmission systems, power levels and wheel arrangements, orders for 174 locomotives being placed by November 1955. For the latter, an experimental prototype was followed by five 'test' classes, which – like the diesels – were produced by a number of builders, including BR itself.

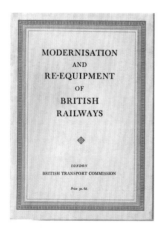

Above left: The 'Modernisation Plan', published at the very end of 1954.
Above right: Modernisation could mean destruction. For some, this was typified by the demolition of the Doric Arch at Euston from the end of 1961. Despite a preservation campaign that featured the poet John Betjeman, the structure was swept away as the station was upgraded during the West Coast Main Line electrification scheme.

Did you know?

BR inherited over 20,000 locomotives, 56,000 coaches, 1 million wagons, 43,000 road vehicles ... and almost 9,000 horses. These fine animals had been a source of motive power since the dawn of railways, but were used latterly for shunting in yards where the use of an engine was not considered economical. The last in service – 'Charlie' – was retired from Newmarket in 1967.

Many drivers and firemen saw that the life they knew was ending. Soon, they'd either leave or learn to love the change, which did bring more comfort to crews, though perhaps without the heroism and dignity associated with the iron horse. The lensmen of British Pathé, Rank and British Transport Films would waste no time in focusing on the new machines and the greater efficiency they seemed to promise. Yet their work revealed not so much a tale of two cities, as a tale of two railways.

Imagine it's 1960 and you're sitting in cinema-darkness to watch *Blue Pullman*, with its Clifton Parker score and stylish photography. What a vision! What a picture of elegance those beautiful, sleek trains were, and what plush interiors! How wonderful to have gazed

Delivered to BR in 1959 and put into service on the Western and London Midland Regions over the next two years, the Blue Pullmans – though luxurious and beautiful – were also prone to poor riding at speed. Here, a unit prepares to depart Paddington for points west. Work on the riding quality of trains would continue throughout most of the 1960s.

A busy scene at London Waterloo. Though steam still worked in and out of the terminus, the trains in the background are electric, drawing 750 volts (DC) through a third rail to the traction motors via bogie-mounted 'shoes'.

through the double-glazed windows as the countryside flashed by. How wonderful to have summoned the smartly turned-out steward to order a boiled egg and fresh coffee, or – perhaps later – a scotch and water before lunch.

Yes, how wonderful. For many, though, the reality of railways matched more closely the grimier world of *Terminus*, released the following year. Here at Waterloo (though it could have been Euston or Leeds, Edinburgh Waverley, Bristol Temple Meads), was a day-in-the-life of the

A 'Blue Train' arriving at Craigendoran in August 1962. Despite early teething problems, these electric multiple units soon settled to give sterling service, proving popular with passengers until withdrawal in 2002.

harried commuter, missing the Tube as the train was late, the little boy lost, the lost umbrellas, the tramps, the travellers, the smuts in eyes, the dirty waiting rooms, fusty carriages ...

Still, a cleaner future was on the way, what with more diesel locomotives being accepted to traffic, and electric services starting between Manchester and Crewe, Liverpool Street and Southend, and round the Glasgow suburbs, where those other 'Blue Trains' were pleasing passengers with their pneumatically operated doors and large windows. At least, they were when their transformers weren't exploding, an issue that forced an embarrassing return to steam for an embarrassing length of time. Fire too could be a problem for many of the diesel types on trial – and there certainly *were* many, the imprudence of ordering such a number of different designs flaring as training and maintenance costs went up and availability came down.

Elsewhere, work was under way on a number of new marshalling yards; that most would take over two years to complete – at a time when freight traffic was falling – summed up for many the Modernisation Plan's expensive distance from reality.

Though passenger receipts rose by £2 million and operating costs had fallen in 1959, competition from domestic airlines and private motor cars was growing. The Commission had been striving to save money by expanding its fleet of multiple units and railbuses, and by closing loss-making lines, but it wasn't enough: in 1960, Macmillan told the House of Commons that 'the railway system must be remodelled to meet current needs, and the Modernisation Plan must be adapted to this new shape'. In a move that doubtless surprised some, Macmillan, a former GWR director, put his faith in Ernest Marples, a contractor involved in motorway construction. To avoid any conflict of interest, the new Transport Minister divested himself of his shares in Marples, Ridgeway ... to his wife. In time, he would be accused of misconduct. In time, he would flee the country. For now, he and his colleagues shared a positive attitude to road building.

Robertson stood firm on the Modernisation Plan, wanting to march on with it; Marples appointed Stedeford and his committee to find ways of reducing its expense. Although he announced that the group's task would be 'to examine the structure, finance and working of the organisations at present controlled by the Commission', its businessmen and civil servants felt

The English Electric Type 5 Deltics began to appear in 1961. In all, twenty-two were built to replace steam on East Coast Main Line expresses. Their 100-mph maximum speed allowed services on the route to be accelerated considerably. Here, D9004 – soon to be named *Queen's Own Highlander* – moves on to King's Cross station in September 1962.

BR inherited a number of ships from the 'Big Four' pre-nationalisation companies and continued to operate ferries to the Channel Islands, Isle of Wight and France, among other destinations. This 1962 timetable details the 'sea services' it provided between Britain and Northern Ireland.

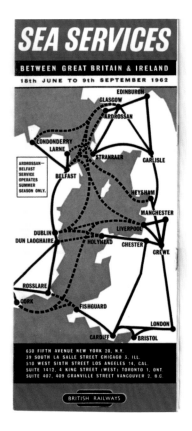

there'd been far too great a focus on engineering. Of the 120 projects the BTC submitted for consideration, electrifying the West Coast Main Line proved the most controversial, one committee member believing it to be a waste of funds, Stedeford himself being more sympathetic to the Commission's cause.

In the event, Stedeford's own view prevailed, though his group's proposals did lead (*inter alia*) to the cancellation of some smaller electrification schemes and the scrapping of centralised signalling on the Nuneaton–Crewe route (which meant the retention of around twenty smaller signal boxes – although the signals they controlled were upgraded to electric colour lights). Robertson was critical and commented on the 'chasm of difference' between his view of the railway as a public service and the government's idea of it as a mere transport competitor. But Robertson was due to retire at the end of May 1961, and the appointment of a Stedeford Committee member as his successor – indeed, the man who'd been so opposed to the electrification plans – was a clear sign that Whitehall wished to take the commercial line.

It had to be said that Dr Richard Beeching was more relaxed than Robertson, and courteous almost to the point of being friendly. For the journalist Anthony Sampson, he might have been 'mistaken at first for one of those large phlegmatic men who tell long stories over a pint of beer in a country pub', but as technical director of ICI, he had the sort of sharp business brain that Marples sought, and which – it was hoped – could solve a problem that had persisted since the nineteenth century: making the railways pay.

Beeching knew this could only be done by analysing the figures and soon authorised a thorough study to assess which traffic ran at a profit, which ran at a loss, which lines made money, and which existed through subsidy alone. He also simplified Robertson's complex management structure of 'generals', committees and sub-committees, opting to recruit private-sector experts in a move to bring financial – as opposed to military – discipline to the organisation. Among these, Philip Shirley (an Australian accountant, late of Unilever) was brought in to increase the Commission's cost consciousness, while Sir Steuart Mitchell (whom Beeching had met at the Ministry of Supply during the war) was charged with rationalising and centralising the railway's Workshops Division. Coupled with this was an acceleration in the run-down of steam, with 1962 seeing almost 3,000 locomotives taken out of service, among which were not only the ex-GWR Kings, which dated from 1927, but also some of the BR Standard designs introduced the decade before.

Electrification of the Crewe–Liverpool Lime Street section of the West Coast Main Line was completed in January 1962. Here, E3017 arrives at Lime Street with an express as a local service departs. Note the overhead wires, from which 25kV AC power is collected by the pantograph on top of the locomotive.

In 1962, BR had twenty-eight workshops in operation. All were well-versed in steam technology, but their experience of modern traction was limited. BR's Workshop Plan, published that same year, outlined a programme of rationalisation and modernisation, including the provision of new plant and machine tools. Swindon Works, seen here in the mid-1960s, was one of those deemed suitable for retention.

By this time, the writing was also on the wall for the BTC itself: the Transport Act of 1962 – while easing BR's burden of debt – did away with the Commission, did away with its Area Boards, and set up five separate bodies in their stead. One of these was the British Railways Board (BRB), which was granted powers to set passenger fares, and more freedom with freight rates than hitherto. Beeching became its first chairman on 1 January 1963. Two months later, Her Majesty's Stationery Office published *The Reshaping of British Railways*, which set out his plan to put the railway 'in the black' by 1970. For some, it was just what the industry needed. For others, it didn't even look good on paper.

Dr Richard Beeching at Laira diesel depot, Plymouth, in 1963.

Did you know?

Born in 1913, Beeching was the son of a journalist. Educated at Maidstone Grammar School, he went on to earn a first in physics at Imperial College, London, gaining his doctorate for research into electrons. During the Second World War, he worked in armaments for the Ministry of Supply, joining ICI in 1947. The analytical mind he brought to BR came at a cost, Beeching's ICI salary of £24,000 a year being matched. This was £14,000 more than his predecessor, and £10,000 more than the Prime Minister – an absolute fortune for the time.

3
What's in a Name?

Lists. So many lists. Lists of royals, lists of flowers, lists of birds, lists of military men. Lists. Well, if you open these things up to the staff, you're going to get exactly what you've got – old names, new names, patriotic names, place names, the odd silly one. But in the Western Region's offices at Paddington, the disparate many are bringing despair to the few. The men of the 'modernisation section', Fred Pugh, Fred Richens and Norman Church, are trying to make sense of it all, trying to find a link. Heads are scratched, coffee is made, the floor is paced. Listening as she types, Mary Weller ponders. Mary Weller smiles. Getting up from her desk, she smiles again.

'Why don't you call them all "Western" something?'

'That's it ... that's the answer!'

And so, the WR's stylish D1000s became known by Mary's elegant prefix. Soon, their twin-engined 90-mph capability would speed services between Paddington and Wolverhampton. Soon, the famous 'Deltics' would do the same for the East Coast Main Line, taking 'The Flying Scotsman' the 392.7 miles from London to Edinburgh in just six hours – an hour faster than before. Before the diesels came. Before electrification came elsewhere.

But as time was being saved for some, it was running out for others, Beeching being an advocate of both accelerating services *and* the abolition of steam. As 1962 became 1963, the number of coal-fired engines on BR's books fell from 11,700 to under 8,000, as the company realised that withdrawing whole classes of locomotive could cut crew, coal, maintenance and stores costs.

As *Reshaping* clarified, though, Beeching understood that improving the financial picture was about more than replacing one sort of traction for another. He understood too that the industry had emerged from the Second World War in 'a poor physical state', that its economic situation had steadily worsened and that the Modernisation Plan failed because it did not predict 'any basic changes in the scope of railway services or in the general mode of operation of the railway system'. And though BR had lost its 'common carrier' status, Beeching felt the company was still 'heavily influenced' by it, focusing on wagonloads (which involve much transhipment and shunting) instead of trainloads (which involve little or none). Road hauliers were much shrewder about selecting lucrative work; BR, on the other hand, took *anything*, even if it yielded no profit.

And profit was key, for, while Beeching recognised that profitability was not the only measure of value for a public service, 'the real question was whether you, as owners of the railways, want us to go on running these services at very high cost, when the demand for them has very largely disappeared'. He thought not, and advocated 'radical changes', recommending that loss-making stations be shut and stopping trains, whose 'overall loss [was] nearly twice receipts', be suspended.

In his thinking, Beeching was echoing *The Organisation of British Transport*, a pamphlet produced by the British Transport Commission soon after nationalisation, which saw that railways were best suited to long distances and large loadings, while roads fared better with short journeys and smaller loadings.

Did you know?

The D1000s were diesel-hydraulic locomotives, meaning that they used a torque converter to convey power (via gears) from the engine to the wheels.

In 1953, BR decided to test a pool of 'hydraulics', in order to measure performance against diesel-electric machines (in which the engine is connected to a generator that creates the power to drive the traction motors). The Western Region agreed to host the trials. Though the D1000s and some of their counterparts were largely successful, all regions bar the Western were equipped to maintain diesel-electrics, which were also cheaper to build and maintain. In 1965, BR decided that the latter were the most suitable for its operating conditions. Withdrawals of the former thus began, the last diesel-hydraulic being taken out of service in February 1977.

Pruning the network had been explored by the Commission too: between 1949 and 1962 it had closed some 3,000 miles of 'unremunerative' lines, but it was Beeching's plan to close 6,000 miles more that drew most attention from the press. Vicky – cartoonist of the *Evening Standard* – had already shown him as an axe-wielding rationaliser, but now television and newspaper reporters pounced on the many protest marches, the 'last rites' ceremonies

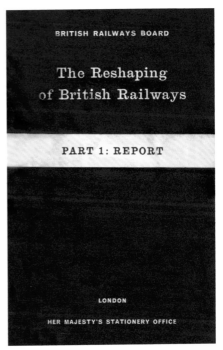

Above left: Brand-new D1037 *Western Empress* receives an oil lamp at Paddington in September 1962. The design team used by BR considered several livery ideas for this class, before 'carriage maroon' was adopted as standard.

Above right: Beeching's infamous first report, published in March 1963.

held as trains departed little-used stations for the last time, and the villagers foretelling the hardship that would come with the withdrawal of services. Comedy duo Flanders and Swann lamented the loss of Audlem, Midsomer Norton and Windmill End in song, and the National Union of Railwaymen published its own report, which warned that '[c]losures in known areas of unemployment [would] throw more people on to the open labour market – and the dole', while pointing to the 'weaknesses', 'errors' and 'guesswork' throughout the analysis.

The trouble was Beeching's income figures were based on receipts issued at a specific place. This painted a gloomier picture for stations more likely to be journey's end than journey's source – not good news for seaside resorts like Lyme Regis or Robin Hood's Bay.

Did you know?

Among the steam locomotives withdrawn in 1963 was No. 60103 *Flying Scotsman*, a Gresley-designed Pacific built for the London & North Eastern Railway in 1923, which holds the distinction of being the first steam locomotive to travel at an authenticated 100 mph.

Its final run came on 14 January, after which it was purchased for preservation by businessman Alan Pegler. Now part of the National Collection, it was re-certified for main-line charter work in 2016.

Traditional 'wagonload' freight operations are evident in this view, as Stanier 8F No. 48371 takes a mixed train over Goyt Viaduct, near Marple, *c.* 1963. BR's pre-Beeching 'common carrier' status meant that it could refuse no consignment, no matter how unprofitable.

He also failed to see that branch lines brought business to the core network, overestimated rail's ability to win general goods traffic from roads, and assumed passengers with no local station would drive to the nearest main-line one, instead of making the entire journey by car (as many in fact would). Yet a number of constructive plans did come out of the report, like the 'liner train' concept, which involved the movement of containerised goods in dedicated 'express' services, and the movement of coal in wagons that could be loaded automatically at collieries and unloaded into bunkers, releasing them back to revenue-earning traffic instead of sitting in power station sidings as bunkers themselves. Both ideas would come to fruition; both ideas capitalised on the 'trainload' concept, which BR also had in mind when signing long-term agreements with six of the major oil companies, a deal sweetened by its new 45-ton tankers, which permitted a much higher payload per train.

Alas, Beeching's bad press eclipsed both the positive side of his first report and virtually all of his second, *The Development of the Major Railway Trunk Routes*, which appeared in February 1965, and which set out to show how rail traffic could be concentrated and further investment justified in a bid to develop 'a new railway out of the old'. The figures saw a decline in passenger, wagonload freight and coal traffic offset by a rise in oil, iron and steel and goods carried by 'liner' train. But though there was a projected increase of 60 to 70 per cent in the overall ton-mileage carried by 1984, modern technology and careful diagramming would mean that it could be carried on 3,000 miles of the 7,500-mile network; as such, only those 3,000 'should be selected for future development'.

The idea was that, by concentrating traffic on single routes, the 'route cost per unit carried' could be reduced, and BR could be made more viable. Unfortunately, the report's language could be ambiguous, which made reassurances that the 'unselected', duplicate trunk routes would not be closed seem dubious, especially when one of them – the Great Central line through Leicester, Nottingham and Sheffield – had already been 'condemned' in the *Reshaping* report.

The part played by politics is a recurrent theme in railway history, and soon Beeching would find himself condemned: by the time *Trunk Routes* appeared in print, Labour had been returned to government. Victory for Harold Wilson brought defeat for Beeching, the latter's unpopularity with the unions making his position untenable for the former, particularly as

7F 2-8-0 No.53808 passes through Midsomer Norton with a Nottingham–Bournemouth service. Listed for possible closure by Beeching, the end for the station and the whole Somerset & Dorset line came in March 1966.

Ex-LNER A4 No. 60004 *William Whitelaw* pauses at Auchinleck with a railtour in June 1963. By this time, withdrawals of this most evocative of classes had already begun. 'No. 4' would be one of the last six to be taken out of service in 1966.

Labour's pre-election manifesto had promised to halt 'major rail closures'. Ennobled in the New Year's Honours list, Lord Beeching was out of 222 Marylebone Road and back at ICI by June.

From that day to this, history has remembered the 'axeman', but Beeching's suggested cuts managed only to contain BR's deficit. His legacy was also much wider than bank balances and

After withdrawal from BR, No. 60103 *Flying Scotsman* was returned to one of its LNER numbers – 4472 – and finished in the 'apple green' livery of its pre-nationalisation owner. Here, the famous engine is turned at London Marylebone after a Stephenson Locomotive Society special on 18 April 1964.

Right: Alan Pegler – *Flying Scotsman*'s second post-nationalisation owner (though by no means its last) – is interviewed at Marylebone, also on 18 April 1964.

Below: Not all steam engines were as lucky as *Flying Scotsman*. Here, ex-GWR No. 5035 *Coity Castle* awaits its fate at Swindon Works after withdrawal.

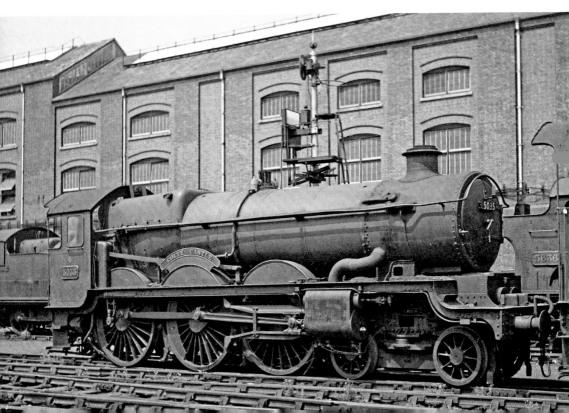

balance sheets, and included improved training programmes, new staff appraisal schemes, up-to-date management methods ... and a new image.

The autonomy afforded to the Regions when the Railway Executive was abolished had let them re-assert their individuality, so – among many other things – the Southern rediscovered the joy of green carriages and the Western returned to its famous 'chocolate and cream'. By 1964, though, it had all started to look a bit faded, a bit dull, a bit 'old hat'.

Beeching had given the company's design team a clear brief to create a sleek, business-like identity that would help bring confidence and cohesion to the network. That May, its initial efforts were revealed when the experimental 'xp64' train was released from Derby Works.

Elsewhere at Swindon, the old is starting to be replaced ever more by the new, as 9F No. 92203 and No. 7808 *Cookham Manor* wait 'on shed' alongside 'Hymek' diesels D7004 and D7087. Thankfully, both steam engines would go on to be preserved.

In the late 1950s, BR began experimenting with four-wheeled diesel railbuses in a bid to cut operating costs and encourage patronage on minor branch lines. In this view, W79977 stands at Cirencester Town, which – unlike some – continued to lose money. The station was earmarked for closure by Beeching and finally lost its passenger service on 6 April 1964.

Representing 'a completely new approach to rail travel comfort and amenity', the carriages featured smarter interiors, better soundproofing, pressure ventilation and improved suspension. Perhaps the most eye-catching element, though, was the livery: a shade of turquoise blue matched with light grey, quite unlike anything that had gone before. The train was hauled by a new Brush Type 4, finished in the same blue, but with one important

Did you know?

In January 1960, the BTC published its requirements for a new breed of 2,500-hp machines, having realised – diesel-hydraulics apart – that the weight of its other classes in that power range was too great, and that the restrictions this imposed on their spheres of operation were unacceptable.

BRCW's winning bid was later rejected amid concerns about the company's reliability. As a result, Brush took the work on, its first Type 4 – D1500 – being completed in September 1962.

Diesel power in evidence at Newcastle in July 1964, in the form of English Electric Types 4 (right) and 5 (left).

addition – there beneath each cab, on a temporary red background, was a striking symbol that would endure beyond its designer's wildest dreams. The final version of the new scheme was revealed at a London exhibition, along with new uniforms, new signage, and a new name: 'British Railways' was dead – long live 'British Rail'.

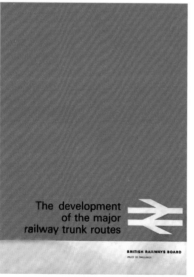

The development of the major railway trunk routes

BRITISH RAILWAYS BOARD

Above: The shape of things to come: 'xp64', hauled by D1733 – one of the new Brush Type 4s. Note the 'arrows of indecision' (as many detractors dubbed BR's new logo).
Left: Beeching's second report, *The Development of the Major Railway Trunk Routes*, published in February 1965.

4
They Think It's All Over ...

Doctor's orders. Some people follow them; some people don't. Others don't like following orders at all. A few, a precious few, know what they're doing and do their best to get on with it. Take Gerry Fiennes, for instance. Fiennes joined the LNER as a traffic apprentice in 1928, and had lived through nationalisation, modernisation and more reorganisation than you could shake a stick at. Believing the lesson that 'when you reorganise, you bleed', Fiennes knew too the three principles of railway work: 'a sense of order, a sense of time, and a sense of money'. In short, he knew how to run a railway. And, as traffic manager on the Eastern Region, he'd seen the virtue of the mighty Deltics early on.

Trials of the powder-blue prototype had begun on the London Midland Region, although at first the manufacturer, English Electric, asked that the locomotive be kept off passenger turns, as they feared the complexity of the 3,300-hp design – and the unreliability of its steam heating boilers – might lead to reputation-damaging repairs in service. While a series of successful freight turns saw *Deltic* put on the 'Merseyside Express' from Liverpool to Euston, it was on the Eastern that the machine made a real impression, not least on Fiennes, who realised it offered the power – and the timetable opportunity – he needed. Some notable performances were recorded between King's Cross and Doncaster, including one memorable morning in February 1960, when the 8.20 – all 250 tons of it – was taken up Stoke Bank at 100 mph. Unfortunately, a serious oil leak later that year would lead to withdrawal the following March. But by then the twenty-two modified production versions were entering service ...

Fast forward to 1965 and timetable opportunities were being sought again. The Eastern still had the Deltics; the London Midland and Southern were electrifying their way to a faster world; but what of the Western? The Western had its Westerns – its

Two production Deltics at Doncaster, the driver of D9001 *St. Paddy* looking back for the guard's flag as D9007 *Pinza* arrives. The photographer's nephew looks on in wonder.

Second best after the Deltics – for Fiennes' Western Region ambitions – was the English Electric Type 3, which began to appear in 1960. Here, D6969 – of 1965 vintage – is seen with classmate D6811 at Wath in March 1966.

English Electric Type 3s D6882 and D6881 leave Paddington for Bristol on 30 May 1966, while a Western waits its turn. The former had been re-geared to increase their maximum permitted speed, though the latter would take over these sped-up services in September 1966.

diesel-hydraulics of varying reliability, with their 90-mph top speeds. Yet the General Manager wanted more; the General Manager was now Fiennes; and Fiennes wanted to try a Deltic on the West of England main line. The engineers reportedly felt it unwise to take one over the steep Devon banks, so he turned to another English Electric product – the Type 3 – or rather, two of them …

So to the spring. So to Paddington. So to the 'Bristolian'. A quarter to nine comes; a green light shines, a guard's whistle blows, a green flag waves. Announcements buzz in the background as lovers wave to lovers, grandparents to children, wives to husbands. In the cab, the driver 'opens up' and an almighty roar resounds around Brunel's great train shed as D6881 and D6882 take the 'xp64' set over the pointwork at the station throat. It was good – very good! – but better would come a few days later.

It's now 3 June, and spring is starting to give way to summer. Imagine being one of the hundred. One of the hundred guests invited to attend a special high-speed run from Paddington to Plymouth. You take your place in one of the nine blue-and-grey coaches as the technicians take theirs in the track recording car. As they prepare the equipment, you sit back in a Second Class saloon. Not for you the blue-and-green moquette; not for you the 'No Smoking' section. The yellow, grey and blue wool upholstery wraps around you and you light another Embassy as the same two Type 3s take their 360-ton train out past Westbourne Park, bound for Old Oak Common and beyond. By the time you get back, there'll have been an unofficial top speed of 104 mph, a thrilling acceleration from 55 to 93 in just 1½ miles at Hemerdon, and the golden 'ton' held in a vice-like grip between Steventon and Goring. It was no record attempt, but a serious attempt to improve things for passengers. The crew were pleased. The technicians were pleased. Fiennes was pleased.

The Western's new '100-mph' timetable came into effect from 18 April 1966 – the same day that electric-hauled services began between Euston, Manchester and Liverpool Lime Street. Such were the hopes for the latter that Henry Johnson (General Manager of the London Midland Region) asked well-known railway author O. S. Nock to write a book on them. He hoped Nock would approve. Nock certainly did.

Published that year, *Britain's New Railway* delighted in the fact that, at one time, 'a journey between London and Liverpool, or London and Manchester, would have been considered as "long-distance" travel; but in this era, when cities such as Zurich or Rome are within two hours' flying time to London airport the new railway services have been geared to the tempo

A young couple enjoying the splendour of their First Class compartment, c. 1966. By now, BR had adopted the continental twenty-four-hour clock, meaning that passengers like these no longer caught the 'Night Ferry' to Dover at nine, but at the seemingly incomprehensible 21:00.

of this modern age.' And it *was* a modern age, this white-heat-of-technology-age, where suddenly all the disruptions suffered while the wires were going up seemed worthwhile.

By this time, Beeching had been replaced by long-term public servant Stanley Raymond. Like Fiennes, Raymond didn't agree with *all* the 'doctor's orders'. Like Fiennes, he didn't have much time for reorganisations, which had created – for him – an 'apparent lack of co-ordination'. What he did have was a vision of how the railway should be developed, and a refusal to accept defeat in the face of road and air competition. Keen to refine BR's marketing strategy, he also fought to build a nationwide 'brand' with a clear identity. Thus in 1966, 'Motorail' became the new name of BR's car-carrying passenger service and 'Inter-City' became synonymous with comfortable, crack expresses. The Deltics fitted this image perfectly; the Type 3s and the electrified West Coast Main Line did too. Steam, however, did not; and one line in particular had relied on it more than most,

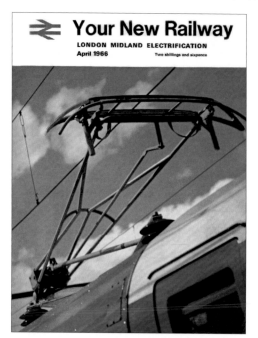

Left: The cover of *Your New Railway*, a special booklet produced by British Rail to mark the start of electric-hauled Inter-City services from Euston in 1966.
Below: The old and the new at Liverpool Lime Street: ex-LMS Black Five No. 45272 waits at the buffer stops alongside AL6 E3109. The latter was one of a hundred locomotives built after tests undertaken with five 'pilot' classes.

one line whose end suggested that Labour's pre-election promise to 'stop Beeching in his tracks' might not be honoured for all.

Back in 1962, if you'd waited on the platform at Midford, you might have seen a plume of smoke, heard a rising rhythm, felt the earth move as *Evening Star* powered the 'Pines Express' through the platform. If you'd come back four years later – on 6 March 1966 – you'd have seen the signalmen – Percy Savage and Harry Wiltshire – polishing the brasswork and wooden floor, just as they'd always done. Except that 6 March 1966 was the last day of the Somerset & Dorset.

Twenty-six miles of the route were single track, which created operational difficulties during the summer months when a large number of holiday services were run each Saturday, most of which required a pilot engine to help them over the steep Mendip gradients. Indeed, it was these uphill struggles – many at 1 in 50 – that created legends. Consider Donald Beale. When he joined in 1919, the S&D was still an independent company. He stayed with the line

Sporting an early version of BR's new blue livery, Sulzer Type 4 D105 is seen at Staveley with a freight in 1966.

BR Standard Class 4 No. 80043, suitably decorated with a 'Farewell S & D' board, leaves Wellow for Templecombe with the 16.25 ex-Bath Green Park on 5 March 1966.

after the Grouping, when the Southern Railway assumed responsibility for infrastructure and signalling, and the LMS led the locomotive side. By the 1950s, he'd climbed the grades to become a Top Link driver, seizing on the local challenge that a late arrival at Bath should be 'Right Time Bournemouth' – a challenge S&D men usually met by pushing that alchemic mix of man, machine and mineral to its height.

In 1956, British Transport Films shot its famous training short *Single Line Working* on part of the route. Among the players was Norman Down, stationmaster at Binegar, who'd play an active part in trying to prevent the line's closure the following decade, and would later lament how – in the run-up to the Beeching report – a census of passengers had been taken during a school holiday, thus worsening the outlook unfairly. But though the line was indeed

Did you know?

Originally created in 1862, when the Somerset Central and Dorset Central amalgamated, the Somerset & Dorset Railway never really made any money, the south seemingly eschewing the strategic link it offered between the Bristol and English Channels. Desperate for a solution, the company gambled on extending north from Evercreech to the Midland's outpost at Bath. When this opened in 1874, a substantial increase in traffic did come – but, alas, too late to save the company, which duly leased the line jointly to the Midland and the London & South Western Railway from 1875.

listed by Beeching, the end had arguably begun in 1951, with the closure of the branch from Glastonbury to Wells.

While other S&D twigs followed, *Reshaping* did bring a certain inevitability regarding the Bath–Bournemouth section, on which there'd been no attempt cut costs or boost earnings, and

Another trunk route that closed in 1966 was the 'Great Central'. Here – on 3 September, the last full day of through traffic – ex-LMS Black Five No. 44984 takes water at Rugby Central before continuing with the 17.15 Nottingham Victoria–London Marylebone service.

which remained steam-operated, mechanically signalled and almost fully staffed throughout. After closure came redundancy, destruction, the dole queue. Yet for BR this was yesterday's railway, and yesterday's railway had no place in the bright new world of tomorrow, a world on which another British Transport Film was shining considerable light.

Entitled *The Good Way to Travel*, it was the sixth in a series of films tracing the network's modernisation – and modern it certainly was, what with the swish 'cab simulator' for training drivers, the ticket printer in use at Liverpool Street and the remodelling of Reading, which amalgamated the old Southern station with the old Great Western one to ease the passage of passengers heading from Bristol to Brighton, or Oxford to Redhill.

Did you know?

British Transport Films was established in 1949 to make training films and travelogues exalting the virtues of places that could be reached by public transport. It also produced regular reports on progress against BR's 'Modernisation Plan'. Led by Edgar Anstey until 1974, it worked on behalf of London Transport, British Waterways, Thomas Cook and the coach operator Thomas Tilling, although most of its output was produced on behalf of the BTC. After that organisation ceased in 1963, it made films chiefly for the British Railways Board.

In 1966, BTF won an Academy Award for *Wild Wings*, which featured Peter Scott's Wildlife & Wetland Trust at Slimbridge. It went on making films through the 1970s and early '80s, but switched off its cameras for the last time in 1982.

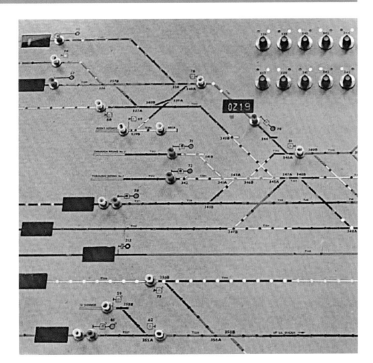

A detail from the impressive control panel at Willesden, taken from *Your New Railway*.

Reading was also used to demonstrate the march of multi-aspect signalling, which brought regularly spaced colour-light signals to allow more trains to be run at higher speeds on the same stretch of line. In this case, a new box replaced twenty-five mechanical ones and controlled the thirty-six miles between Twyford and Uffington, seven miles of the West of England line, ten miles of the Basingstoke line and seven miles between Didcot and Kennington Junction.

Add to this the impressive control room at Willesden, a new cross-Channel ferry, all the automatic point heaters, automatic lubricators and track fault recorders, and it was easy to see how 'the best in ideas, the newest of materials, the most modern methods are being employed to make sure that British Rail becomes undisputedly the good way to travel'. And yet. And yet the accompanying music harked back to an earlier era, an era that was more Shadows than Spencer Davis, more clanking wagons than sleek interiors ...

The opening scene features Tinsley marshalling yard, where – the narrator says – 'the electronic railway age' has 'not only arrived, but settled down'. Opened the previous October, it used the Dowty Wagon Control System of hydraulic rams to either speed or slow wagons rolling from the top of a 'hump' into a huge fan of sidings below. It was the last marshalling yard to be built under the Modernisation Plan and by 1966 it was handling over 24 million tons of goods a year.

Tinsley undoubtedly made freight handling in the Sheffield area more efficient, allowing several smaller marshalling yards to be closed, and limiting the length of time wagons waited in sidings for loading, unloading or transhipment. In *Trunk Routes*, Beeching had seen that 'general merchandise' offered 'very substantial traffic potential', and was expected to have grown some 120 per cent by 1984 ('if an average growth rate in the gross national product of

To propel wagons up to the 'hump' at Tinsley marshalling yard, BR used one of three 'master and slave' shunters. Here, D4502 is seen between duties shortly after the complex opened.

Brush Type 4 D1767 at York with a test train of 'merry-go-round' coal hoppers.

4 per cent per annum is achieved'). In short, Tinsley and its kind seemed to offer the chance of making unprofitable traffic profitable. But in short, Beeching was wrong: wagonload traffic was ebbing as more motorways were built and more road hauliers set up in business; wagonload traffic would never be what it once was.

Still, Beeching's favoured 'block trains' were carrying ever-increasing tonnages and new rolling stock was being built to cater for them. In 1966, a prototype 90-ton bogie tanker was introduced to service with Shell-Mex and BP, while elsewhere work was continuing on the Fiennes-fed 'merry-go-round' network (as he dubbed it), whose trains of new hopper wagons carried coal from colliery to power station, loading and unloading automatically at low speed. From the first full test run in 1965, conversions had continued apace to the extent that, by the end of the following year, around 900 wagons were carrying 53,000 tons of black gold a week to four installations.

This brighter block train future also featured in *The Good Way to Travel*, where cement trains, trains of powdered limestone and car panels for Vauxhall were shown slicing through the landscape, their speeds higher, their efficiency greater than their older counterparts, thanks to a combination of new traction, new rolling stock and new continuous welded rail, laid – as the film also showed – mechanically in a manner so much better than 'the flat-footed methods of yesterday'. So perhaps rail really was 'the good way' for people *and* goods to travel. Perhaps the electronic railway age really had settled down. Perhaps.

5
... It Is Now

It's the last day of July 1967. It's just after half-two and a freight is pulling in to Skelton en route from Cliffe to Uddingston. It's a regular turn, a 'block train', the sort of train that would've made Beeching proud. The guard exchanges greetings with the man about to take over. A wagon examiner plies his trade, but the new guard looks at the couplings himself. Towards the rear of the rake he finds a slack one, tightens it up and prepares for the off. When it comes, he settles so he can keep an eye on things from the brake van's ducket window. He always does this for cement trains; cement trains – or at least the new 'Cemflo' wagons – can be trouble ...

... and shortly after 3.15 p.m. trouble comes as one wagon starts to sway, its movement increasing until its wheels leave the rails near Thirsk. To the guard, it looks like a bulge, but quickly becomes much more as a coupling breaks and eight wagons disappear down the embankment. All but one come to rest clear of the adjacent line. All but one ...

Looming large on that line is the 12.00 King's Cross to Edinburgh, its driver enjoying a clear run after a temporary – frustrating – speed restriction near Tollerton. He could be powering up; he should be able to see the next signal. He can't. Something's in the way. A mist? A haze? He closes the locomotive's controller, but as he starts to apply the brake, out of the haze comes

The locomotive hauling the passenger train involved in the fatal collision at Thirsk was DP2, an experimental Type 4 built by English Electric. It was so badly damaged that it had to be withdrawn.

Did you know?

Thirsk was not the only fatal rail accident to occur in this period. At Hither Green on 5 November 1967, for example, a passenger train derailed on a piece of broken rail, killing forty-nine people. Though the cause was the way in which the track had been supported, it was realised more generally that the smaller wheels of diesel and electric locomotives and units, combined with the high unsprung weight resulting from their axle-hung traction motors, had a more damaging effect on the track than was evident with steam.

On 6 January 1968, a huge road transporter carrying a 120-ton transformer was struck by an express at Hixon Automatic Half-Barrier level crossing. Eleven people were killed. The driver had not telephoned the signalman, as required by the instructions for use. Later, he would claim he believed his safe passage had been assured by the fact his police escort had crossed ahead of him.

The subsequent Court of Inquiry found that the haulier had failed to inform BR that it intended to take the transporter over the crossing, which in turn prevented BR from taking appropriate precautions. It also found (*inter alia*) that communications between both railway and police and railway and haulier about the need to inform the signalman in such cases had been poor.

the wagon. He throws out all the anchors. He works the sander to aid adhesion. His secondman gets three detonators ready to protect the line if they survive. If ...

... the wagon tears into the side of the locomotive and six of the carriages. The sound is excruciating, but they're alive to hear it. Not so seven of the passengers.

Soon on the scene was Gerry Fiennes, by now General Manager of the expanded Eastern Region, which had swallowed up its North Eastern neighbour at the start of the year. The selfless behaviour of the express crew impressed him so much that he lent them his car so they could get home. Less impressive though were the wagons, which had started to appear from 1961, and had been blighted by problems with broken springs and underframe cracks, so much so that their permitted speed had been cut from 60 mph to 45 when laden. Tests also showed that 'hunting'– a strange lateral wheel oscillation – could develop at around 25 mph and was exaggerated if couplings were slack. The guard's unease had been well founded.

Not that the 'Cemflo' wagons involved at Thirsk were alone in their apparent tendency to jump from the rails. Indeed, freight train derailments were becoming an unnerving theme. There had been 259 in 1966 alone, most involving the traditional short wheelbase wagon and occurring not on pointwork but plain line. These combinations had been a relatively trouble-free part of the railway for years, but modernisation had brought in more steel-framed wagons, which – while easier to maintain – intensified the 'hunting' phenomenon, being less flexible than their older counterparts and therefore more prone to a build-up of oscillations after any imperfections in the track. Though not a feature of Thirsk itself, CWR – 'continuously welded rail' – could introduce even more rigidity, while its lack of joints meant fewer natural breaks to disrupt the effect. When these factors combined with the sustained, more immediate, high speeds possible with diesel traction and through braking, incidents increased alarmingly.

English Electric Type 1s D8301 and D8302 stand outside York shed in 1967. It had been the lack of visibility for crew when working 'bonnet-first' that led to the design's initial fall from favour before its superiority over the Clayton offering (see page 53) became apparent.

BR Chairman Stanley Raymond and the Transport Minister discuss 'Motorail' matters at a March 1967 exhibition. Their ways would part later in the year.

Above: By 1967, the block trains advocated by Beeching were starting to replace many traditional goods services. Here, Brush 4 D1635 nears Beattock Summit with a 'Freightliner' that June.
Below right: The book that ended Gerry Fiennes's career, as noted in the text.

The solution was being sought by the Research Division, which developed a programme headed by Alan Wickens, who had been recruited from the aerospace industry specifically to consider the problem. His team – which included many other aerospace engineers – devised a new suspension system that could achieve a good quality ride at all speeds on any type of track. The understanding gained from this work was also applied to bogie vehicles in 1967, and materialised in the 'Mark III' coach, which was capable of 125 mph. This step forward would be part of the future, but it was a future Fiennes (for one) did not wish to see.

Fiennes was sixty-one in 1967, four years from retirement. The previous year he had written that he did not want to get involved in this higher-speed railway, or with the container age. There just wasn't enough time left in his career to do anything meaningful about any of it.

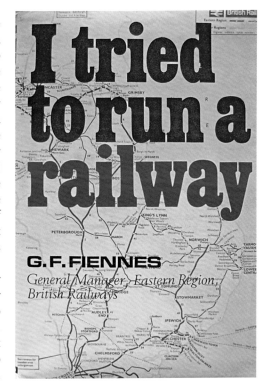

He also confessed himself 'thoroughly bored by reorganisations' and 'being lectured [to] by the British Railways Board'. Unfortunately, he was writing not in a private diary, but a book published that September. It was called *I Tried to Run a Railway*. Stanley Raymond was not amused. Fiennes closed the door on his way out. Not that Raymond had much time left either.

Ironically, Raymond's own hands had helped seal his own fate. More ironically, his motivation shared something with the way Fiennes viewed the world. Both men, after all, did not want all of Beeching's proposed line closures to come to pass. In 1964, Fiennes had argued the case to keep the Clevedon, Minehead and Padstow branches open, pointing out that their direct costs did not greatly exceed revenue, and that their contributory revenue was comparatively large. HQ didn't agree. Two years later, though, HQ – in the form of Raymond – explained to Transport Minister Barbara Castle that, while Beeching's proposed 8,000-mile network was a reduction too far, dropping to 11,000 would be far more appropriate.

Castle proposed a working party to consider the question in the round. Raymond reckoned the matter should be looked at by the Board and the Ministry together and thus a Joint Steering Group was born, with a view to identifying the 'social cost' of the railway and setting BR realistic financial targets. Not that the 'JSG' was entirely made up of ministers and railwaymen, Castle insisting that independent consultants be added to the mix, so that it would be 'accepted politically as a genuine exercise' for the good of the railway. Some – London Midland General Manager Henry Johnson among them – smelled a rat, and thought Raymond should have insisted on chairing the group himself. In the event, Castle saw to it that thirty-five-year-old parliamentary secretary John Morris took up that position. In July 1967, however, Johnson's fears came true when Morris told Castle that Raymond was incapable of bringing the changes to management culture and practice that BR so badly needed.

By this time, other changes were afoot, as the new railway – with its new liveries, new uniforms and new advertising campaigns – was starting to take hold. But while many stations retained their traditional benches, barrows and signs, the fires were fading fast.

BR Standard Class 4 No. 80012 shunts old and new liveried stock at Clapham Junction towards the end of steam on the Southern Region.

The first region to rid itself of steam had been the Western, Scotland saw it go in June, but the last to use it on express passenger trains was the Southern, which had opted to withdraw engines as it electrified route by route. While the third rail was being laid alongside the Waterloo–Bournemouth line, therefore, most trains remained in the charge of Oliver Bulleid's mighty Pacifics, which – while expensive to work and maintain – were highly impressive; those rebuilt in the 1950s enjoyed increased efficiency, leaving Southern managers certain they'd be able to handle most traffic needs until electrification was complete.

Rebuilt Bulleid Battle of Britain No. 34089 *602 Squadron* powers through Clapham Cutting in June 1967. The white headcode discs denote the type of train being worked – classic Southern practice.

Battersea power station looms in the background, as rebuilt Bulleid West Country No. 34034 takes on water at Nine Elms depot in 1967. Though the nameplate – *Honiton* – is missing, the fire will burn a little while longer.

Some Southern drivers were looking forward to the comparative comfort of the cab after years on the footplate, but for a large number the summer was tinged with sadness: they knew the end was coming; they knew they might soon join the unemployed; they gave it everything, their last hurrah resulting in logbooks full of astounding performances. Many steam fans, photographers and home-movie enthusiasts relished the sight of the old engines as they thundered past, their green retinue broken only by the odd flash of blue and grey. Among them was a man more famous for his paintings of elephants – David Shepherd – who positioned himself at Nine Elms depot to capture the final hours of the great beasts in their natural surroundings. As soot and grime fell on artist and canvas, it became part of the picture, preserved forever, as Shepherd's own two locomotives – Nos 92203 and 75029 – soon would be.

Out on the main line, the magic 'ton' was reached on several occasions but, when No. 35003 *Royal Mail* touched 105.88 mph between Winchfield and Fleet as it worked a train from Weymouth on 26 June, it was the last time a steam locomotive performed that feat in Britain. All-too-soon the end came and went, leaving the new order to take over from Monday 10 July. But while electrification brought sleeker services and higher passenger numbers, it also condemned Southern spotters to a diet of bland multiple units, which did little to stir the blood. They weren't exactly state-of-the-art, either: the SR had chosen to base its front-line trains on the 1950s Mark I carriage at a time when the other regions were taking delivery of new Mark IIs (although the units were more up-to-date than the forty-year-old Tube stock that had replaced steam on the Isle of Wight, it had to be said).

After the withdrawal of steam, Waterloo–Bournemouth services were taken over by electric multiple units like this one, seen at the Dorset resort in 1967.

Did you know?

A lack of funds for electrifying beyond Bournemouth created the need for an efficient way of changing traction for the run to Weymouth. The solution led to a combination of push-pull operation and an ingenious method of working, whereby non-powered carriages were propelled by a '4-REP' electric multiple unit from Waterloo to the Dorset resort. Here, the 'REP' would be uncoupled and an adapted BRCW Type 3 would hook on and haul the train the rest of the way. The diesel would then push the carriages back to Bournemouth where the waiting 'tractor unit' would take over for the return to London. Services began in June 1967 and would last until the third rail reached Weymouth in the late 1980s.

BRCW Type 3 D6517– adapted for 'push-pull' working, as mentioned in the text – passes St Denys.

For BR's publicity department, the death of steam on the Bournemouth line had made travel 'clean, quiet, fast and frequent' – 'fit for the '70s', in fact. No longer would there be 'muck everywhere'. No longer would it get 'in your eyes, your ears, in your hair'. No longer would smoke obscure the beauty of Bournemouth or the majesty of Winchester. Yet not everyone welcomed all the changes and, as the gap between past and present grew, the preservation movement started to grow teeth. And it wasn't just about saving steam engines – BR's intention to 'develop' St Pancras and King's Cross (which would result in the destruction of at least one architectural gem) was a case in point: having failed in his bid to save Euston's Doric Arch earlier in the decade, poet John Betjeman was quick to join the anti-demolition campaign. This time, there was to be a modicum of success and, after a year of negotiation, St Pancras attained a Grade I listing in November 1967.

Did you know?

His parents having died when he was just six years old, Stanley Raymond was brought up in in an orphanage, the head of which saw his ability and paid for him to attend Hampton Grammar School in Middlesex. After a distinguished war career, he worked with the London Passenger Transport Board and British Road Services, before joining the railway in the mid-1950s. After various roles, he became General Manager of the Western in January 1962. Here, he made a name for himself as a ruthless moderniser.

According to former colleague Michael Bonavia, Raymond's capacity for work 'was prodigious, and this sometimes led him to take on tasks that could well have been left to others'. Knighted in 1967, he refused the chairmanship of the Freight Integration Council after his ousting from BR by Barbara Castle, later moving to the Horserace Betting Levy Board.

He died in May 1988, aged seventy-four.

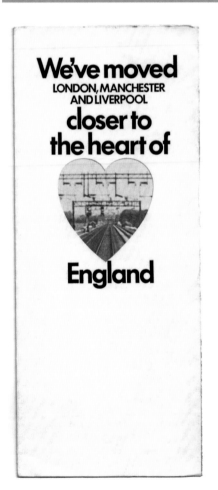

We've moved
LONDON, MANCHESTER AND LIVERPOOL
closer to the heart of
England

By the end of the following month, Raymond had cleared his desk and was gone. The strategies that he – and the JSG – had helped to shape, and that would go on to be galvanised in the seminal 1968 Transport Act, would not come to fruition under his leadership. Castle agreed with her advisors and decided that, while the new policies would give BR 'fresh terms of reference involving a different outlook in matters of finance and long-range planning', they required a corresponding change at the top. Though choosing first to 'force him to resign', she eventually offered Raymond the chairmanship of the Freight Integration Council, a new body she hoped would help knit road and rail transport together. In reality, Raymond wasn't left with much choice. His resignation was readily accepted.

The press speculated that Peter Parker, then director of food wholesaler Booker McConnell, would take over; his time would come – but not yet.

A leaflet produced to promote BR's electric West Coast Main Line services in 1967.

The part-electrified West Coast Main Line remained BR's 'flagship' route. Here, AL1 E3017 – still in 'electric blue' livery – hauls a rake of new corporate 'blue and grey' Mark II stock up Camden Bank, near Euston.

Brand-new English Electric Type 4 D400 waits at Crewe South on 1 November 1967. The locomotive was one of a fleet born from a need to speed up passenger services on the non-electrified section of the West Coast Main Line north of Weaver Junction. All fifty had been delivered by December 1968, by which time a reclassification of all traction types had seen them re-dubbed 'Class 50'.

6

The Old Tradition

In the Somerset town of Radstock, a rumble is heard. A rumble and a clank. Rumble and clank. It's a cold morning, and trees are silvered with frost as you head to the station to see what's going on. No more does the 'Pines' whistle through, no more stoppers for Wellow, Midford and Bath Green Park – not for a couple of years now. No, this is the low throb of a diesel and, as you stand at the closed level crossing gates, you can see it waiting. D7031 – a Hymek, one of the Western's diesel-hydraulics – is an unwelcome visitor to these parts. The cab door opens, and a 'pilot' climbs to the warmth of the cab to help guide the train southwards, where it will eventually stop to reclaim track and other components no longer wanted on this no-longer railway.

Back in 1964, you'd believed the Labour Party candidates when they'd told you that they would stop Beeching 'in his tracks'. You voted. They got in. And the line still closed. So did the Great Central through Leicester, Nottingham and Sheffield. So did seemingly countless branch lines. You felt despondent. You felt betrayed. But now – in 1968 – things seem to be changing. Some stations – like Looe and St Ives – have already been saved, and the logic behind the reprieves has been embodied in a new Transport Act, which will draw a distinction between BR's commercial sector and its socially desirable (but unprofitable) side.

The 1968 Act was the fourth major piece of legislation since the war, its main aim being to put the industry on a greater public service footing. This meant it not only wiped out BR's debt of £153 million, but also established Passenger Transport Executives (PTEs) in and around Greater Manchester, Glasgow, Merseyside, Tyneside and the West Midlands. The idea was that the PTEs would co-ordinate local bus and rail services, 'purchasing' the latter from BR on a contract basis. Grants were also available for the 'social' railway, including £400,000 for Paddington–Oxford services, £2.5 million for Glasgow North and South suburban services and £9 million for Southern Region commuter traffic.

Hymek D7031 waits in the platform at Radstock North before heading down to the track lifting site on the former Somerset & Dorset line. The shunter – D3185 – waits for the level crossing gates to open to allow it to leave with the coal it has brought in from Writhlington Colliery.

In 1968, the Western Region starting double-heading certain West of England trains in a bid to improve the timetable. Here, Warships D867 *Zenith* and D869 *Zest* enter Exeter St David's with a Penzance service.

Did you know?

In 1965, J. F. Harrison (BR's Chief Engineer, Traction and Rolling Stock) realised that the time would come when BR would need a single 4,000-hp traction unit, which would require less maintenance than a twin-engined vehicle and do away with the need to double-head some freight trains.

HS4000 *Kestrel* was built in 1967 by Brush Traction of Loughborough to demonstrate the viability of Harrison's idea and promote possible export orders. The 133-ton machine was fitted with a 4,000-hp Sulzer engine, which provided a maximum speed of 125 mph.

Ceremonially handed over to BR at Marylebone station in January 1968, it was officially allocated to Tinsley depot, though spent most of its time at Shirebrook. Test runs were conducted with passenger and freight stock, although the latter predominated (especially on coal trains between Mansfield and Whitemoor Yard).

It was taken out of service in March 1971 and later sold to the Soviet Union, where it gave almost twenty years of service before withdrawal in 1989.

In 1968, Brush Traction's experimental diesel-electric *Kestrel* was handed over to BR for testing. It had the requisite 4,000-hp engine for 125-mph running, but was too heavy to be driven faster than 100 mph. Withdrawn in 1971, it was later sold to the Soviet Union.

Work-weary Black Five No. 45255 leaves Manchester Exchange with a parcels train on 9 March 1968. The locomotive would be withdrawn later in the year; the station would be closed in 1969, its remaining services being transferred to Manchester Victoria.

By the time the Act received royal assent on 25 October, Castle too had been replaced – by Richard Marsh, formerly of the Ministry of Power, a self-professed motorist, but one whose father had worked for the Great Western at Swindon. His private personal secretary – though unbeknown to him initially – also happened to be the daughter of Henry Johnson, the new chairman of BR. The latter was a career railwayman who had started his working life with the LNER, and who went on to become General Manager of the Eastern and London Midland Regions. Popular with staff, Johnson was a true motivator and had a greater grasp of engineering matters than all who had gone before him. He was also a man sitting on the fulcrum of change.

In the twenty years since nationalisation, BR's route mileage had shrunk from 20,000 to less than 11,000, staff numbers had dropped from nearly 650,000 to 296,000, and wagon numbers had fallen from over a million to just 430,000. Indeed, freight had perhaps fallen the furthest. The Modernisation Plan had foreseen the growth of container traffic, BR testing

Visitors view the mix of steam and diesel at Stockport Edgeley shed on a rainy Saturday 27 April 1968. The depot closed for good a week later.

the water with its 'Condor' and (later) 'Speedfreight' services. Beeching took the idea forward with the liner concept, which – while successful – made many new marshalling yards redundant. Around 800 were closed, but, while Freightliner established itself as a national network (even extending its reach to France and Belgium), BR felt there was still business to be had in the sundries market.

The Act would see a major shareholding in Freightliner and the unremunerative small-consignment collection and delivery service transferred to a new National Freight Corporation. Though some managers were unhappy, this could be good for the balance sheet but, if BR were to compete for sundries on a serious level, it would have to reorganise the way its rolling stock was managed. The computer system that could deliver this was coming, but in the meantime sales activity was damped down until service quality could match the quality of the new air-braked wagons that were being developed.

Did you know?

In a bid to combat the 'hunting' problem so vividly highlighted by the Thirsk accident, BR's Research Division developed a High Speed Freight Vehicle to demonstrate its work into wheel-rail dynamics practically. The first variant – HSFV-1 – was built in 1966 and was soon followed by others, HSFV-3 being a converted Cemflo wagon built in direct response to Thirsk.

By 1968, HSFV-4 – a converted ferry van – was under test and would prove the practicality of running long-wheelbase two-axle wagons at speeds of up to 75 mph. The first – air-braked – wagons of this type started to appear in 1969 and would go on to feature in BR's 'Air Braked Network' – later renamed 'Speedlink'.

On the passenger side, the Western had improved its timetable by double-heading on the 'Cornish Riviera' between Paddington and Penzance, while the Scottish Region was seeking to speed up services between Glasgow and Edinburgh by similar means. But for all this, and for all British Transport Films' claims that the electrified Bournemouth line was ready for the coming decade, it was the lines out of Euston that remained BR's flagship 'new railway'.

Shortly before the Queen approved the new Act, she opened the new, rebuilt Euston, telling the crowds that it marked 'the completion of the most important railway modernisation project of this century'. People cheered. People clapped. Not everyone was happy: Betjeman described the station tersely as 'no masterpiece' and said its lack of platform seating made it an 'inhuman structure', which seemed to ignore passengers. BR disagreed and made sure its clean lines and modern signs featured in films, fliers, posters and pamphlets that showed how tickets could be bought in the shiny Travel Centre, coffee and cigarettes enjoyed in the Sprig Buffet, and three-course meals taken in the Lancastrian Grill …

Not that it was electric traction all the way on the 100-mph West Coast Main Line, the wires stopping at Weaver Junction, where the route to Liverpool diverged from the main path to Scotland. The government was unlikely to approve electrification beyond this point, but BR's new English Electric Type 4s were more than capable of taking trains over the punishing gradients of Shap and Beattock. These 'Class 50s' were based on DP2 –

The Travel Centre in the rebuilt Euston, c. 1968. This artist's impression is taken from a booklet BR produced to mark the upgrade.

AL6 E3146 at the new Euston, soon after its official opening.

Class 50 D406 pulls in to Hellifield with a diverted Up express on 4 August 1968.

Nearing the end: Stanier 8Fs. Nos 48666 and 48727 stand out of use at Rose Grove depot on 20 July 1968.

the experimental locomotive which met its end at Thirsk, but with which the Operating Department had been impressed, thanks to its ability to outperform the Deltics while on the East Coast Main Line.

Their on-board circuitry often led to failures, but the 50s proved their worth and added to the prestige of this premier route, where passenger numbers were climbing as the distance between London, Manchester, Edinburgh, Glasgow and Liverpool seemed to shrink. And yet, as the shiny blue locomotives took their shiny new coaches through Carnforth, there couldn't have been a greater contrast with the greying steam engines in this last outpost of the old tradition.

In January 1968, there'd been more than 350 engines still at work in northwest England. Enthusiasts flocked in to watch 8Fs fight with freights, while Black Fives worked local services and shunted the yards. Steam had personality – steam engines *breathed* – and required some effort on the part of their crews to produce the power that ensured you got home after a day in Bradford or that your parcel got to grandad up in Glasgow. The work had brought pride, and that's partly why the engines attracted as many admirers on the job as off it. Old drivers might have jokingly said 'down with steam', but many reminisced about that battle over the moors with a mineral train, while firemen recalled how smoke seemed to linger about engines that had been 'dead' for a month, as they waited in weed-strewn sidings for that fateful trip to the scrapyard.

The final timetabled steam services came on 3 August, the last two of all centring on Preston. As Black Fives Nos 45212 and 45318 arrived from Lostock Hall shed, they were greeted by a flurry of flashbulbs and roars of approval 'more usually reserved for a West Ham goal against Chelsea', as one journalist later put it. At 20.48, the former set off for Blackpool South; at 21.25, the latter made for Liverpool Exchange, where – on arrival – it was serenaded by rousing renditions of 'Auld Lang Syne' and 'God Save Our Gracious Steam'. It was a carnival atmosphere, but a carnival tinged with regret, for – apart from a few specials on the 4th – it was over, the last sheds – Lostock Hall, Carnforth and Burnley's Rose Grove – closing their doors for good. Many of their charges were now well past their best, their numbers barely visible, their paintwork buried under layers of grime. Some enthusiasts had done the best they could with cleaning oil and rags; others found the grime responded well to chalk, and chose instead to adorn tenders and boilers with unofficial slogans like 'steam lives' or 'steam forever'. But nothing lasts forever, and it was left to BR's 'Farewell to Steam' special to close the chapter, if not the book.

Although there is no official headboard, this is the famous 'Farewell to Steam' tour of 11 August 1968, more commonly known as the 'Fifteen Guinea Special' in recognition of its rather exorbitant price. Britannia No. 70013 *Oliver Cromwell* is just backing on to the train at Manchester Victoria, having taken over from Black Five No. 45110.

Fifteen guineas was the price. Fifteen guineas bought you 314 miles of steam, 'luncheon, high tea with refreshments, souvenir tickets and a souvenir scroll'. And so at 09.10 on 11 August, those who could afford it, those who could stand it, settled in their seats as No. 45110 eased the train out of Liverpool Lime Street. Those who couldn't afford it stood and watched; those who couldn't stand it – who couldn't bear to see steam bow out like this – stayed away. At Manchester Victoria some ninety minutes later the Black Five was replaced by a resplendent No. 70013 *Oliver Cromwell*, which took over until Carlisle. When the train

Right: A poster from 1968, showing a young couple reunited by Inter-City.
Below: BR began operating light hovercraft services to the Isle of Wight in 1966. Two years later, it took delivery of the first SRN4, which could handle 250 passengers and thirty cars. Named *The Princess Margaret*, the craft worked between Dover and Boulogne under BR's new 'Seaspeed' brand. A second SRN4 was purchased in 1969 for the Dover–Calais route.

The 'I'll see you again' Train.
Inter-City cuts the distance to distant friends

British Rail *Inter-City*

returned to Liverpool later that day, children cheered, women waved and grown men wept. The end had come.

For BR, steam may have been old-fashioned and inefficient, but so were some of the early diesels, time having already been called on many of the biggest failures to come out of its earlier over-ordering policy. Much of this was about unreliability, but it was also about changing traffic patterns, as trip freights between and branch line services were ebbing in the face of increasing road competition and the resultant 'Beeching cuts'. There was also a need to increase standards of availability and utilisation in BR's move towards containerised 'trainload' freight haulage, and a need to cut staff training and maintenance costs across the board. All this meant more withdrawals as BR aimed to reduce the number of diesels on its books from around 3,000 to just over 2,200 by 1974.

As the 1960s began to close, it wasn't just the railways that were changing. The whole decade had seen consumerism grow to such an extent that car ownership had risen from around 6 million to over 11 million in 1969. Though clearly dominant for short and medium-length journeys, the picture for long-distance travel was slightly different. Yes, the 'sparks effect' had seen custom double since 100-mph trains were introduced on the West Coast Main Line. And yes, the figures for air had dropped by 17 per cent. Now, though, market research had found that, while rail remained the mode of choice for journey times of up to three hours, people tended to prefer the plane for anything longer. Electrification was certainly a solution, and would reduce journey times in the Class 50 domain by 1974, but its expense suggested that – if rail were truly to compete with air – a new train would be needed ...

The winter sun streams onto Deltic D9003 *Meld* and Brush 4 D1868 as they wait at King's Cross in December 1968.

7
The New Tradition

1 January 1969, and the new Transport Act comes in to effect; 1 January 1969, and the National Freight Corporation comes into being; 1 January 1969 and the first year of no steam begins ...

Within a few days, enthusiasts will have something else to mourn, as the 94-mile 'Waverley Route' – the old North British line from Edinburgh to Carlisle, which opened in 1849, which was named after the novels of Sir Walter Scott, which was listed by Beeching – closes for

The last day of the 'Waverley Route' finds Clayton Type 1 D8606 stabled at Hawick due to justified concerns about justifiable public protest. Because of this, the locomotive was run in front of the last scheduled train as far as Newcastleton to ensure the line was free from obstruction.

The Hawick ticket office, closed, in January 1969. An attempt to save the 'Waverley' line by the Border Union Railway Co. Ltd failed, but in 2006 Scottish Parliament passed an act to rebuild and reopen it. As a result, services recommenced as far as Tweedbank (Galashiels) in September 2015.

good. The last train – the sleeper from Edinburgh on the night of 5 January – was delayed at Newcastleton by locked level crossing gates and a mass of villagers about to lose their lifeline. Alas, they could only delay the inevitable for an hour, David Steel MP – who had opposed the closure and who was travelling on board – intervening at one point to secure the train's passage. Freight trundled on for a while longer, but the route – like the Somerset & Dorset and the Great Central before it – was essentially part of history, part of the old railway: defeated ... defunct ... dead.

Still, this was a modern world and there was a modern railway out there, which – while not much use for getting to Radstock, or Quorn or Eskbank – was perfect for going Inter-City to Bristol, Cardiff, Glasgow, Liverpool or Manchester. It was also ideal for getting coal from collieries to power stations, the 'merry-go-round' allowing BR to play its part in bringing electricity to Britain's homes with greater efficiency. Within just two more years there would be twelve power stations equipped with the loop lines, hoppers and discharge gear needed

By the end of the 1960s, many of the less successful diesel designs ordered by BR in the '50s had been withdrawn. Here, one such – North British Type 1 D8402 – awaits its fate at Cohens of Cransley.

Diesel reliability in general had improved by the end of the decade, but that of the Brush Type 2s increased markedly when their ailing Mirrlees engines were exchanged for English Electric ones. The last to be upgraded would be D5500 in 1969. Here, D5501 is seen working a freight at Stratford.

to facilitate this highly effective mode of operation (so effective in fact that a similar system would soon be established at Immingham Docks to speed the flow of imported iron ore to the British Steel plant at Scunthorpe). Oil traffic was on the rise too, with around 18.2 million tons a year being transported in around 12,000 bogie tank wagons, the railway here being less a conveyor belt than a mobile pipeline, able to be set up and put into action wherever it was needed.

Though Raymond had seen Freightliner as 'the brightest jewel in British Rail's crown', the brand had made a loss of £3 million in 1968, making its transfer to the National Freight Corporation more appealing to BR's accountants than its operators. That said, there were seventeen dedicated container terminals by 1968 and, though much of the initial traffic involved short-distance domestic hauls, the situation improved when it was realised that rail was ideal for carrying containers to and from ports. Success with the service between Harwich and Zeebrugge would see Tilbury added to the Freightliner network in 1970, Felixstowe and Southampton (Maritime) following two years later.

The speed of Freightliners, oil trains – trains of all types – was being aided by the spread of multi-aspect colour-light signalling, 1969 seeing the completion of a number of major schemes, including Old Oak Common, Swindon and Gloucester on the Western Region, and Trent, Derby and Saltley on the London Midland. The Old Oak scheme was an extension of the 1962 installation and controlled signals from Paddington to Hayes, allowing eighteen of the old manual boxes to be closed. Together, those opened in 1969 allowed multi-aspect signalling – MAS – to extend from Chesterfield to just west of Reading, across some of the most densely used parts of BR.

Technology was making the modern railway possible. Technology was attracting more business. But would technology be able to fight back against the ever-moving, ever-present, ever-growing threats from private motor car ownership, road coaches and domestic airlines?

BR had tried to bring motoring to the railway through an agreement with Godfrey Davis to provide car-hire facilities at major stations, with New Pudsey – a new type of station, with a large car park that gave motorists access to the Inter-City network without the hassle of city centre parking and congestion – and with the innovative 'Motorail' concept, which allowed passengers to take their cars with them on

Colour light signalling would go on to replace mechanical equipment throughout the 1970s and '80s, with new power signal boxes opening at Bristol (1970), Doncaster (1979) and Leicester (1986), among others. In this official BR view, a Western is passing a junction signal controlled by 'OO' – Old Oak Common.

Above: Deltic D9003 *Meld* heads past Little Wymondley with a London-bound express in 1969 – a classic portrait of BR's contemporary 'corporate' livery.

Below: Despite the new, pockets of the old remained in places, as here at Golspie, where BRCW Type 2 D5336 splutters as the milk and parcels are unloaded.

special wagons, away from congested roads altogether. In July 1969, BR explained that it intended to develop this scheme in the decade ahead. In July 1969, BR explained a lot of things it hoped to achieve in the 1970s, from improving services at its hotels and catering outlets, to increasing its fleet of ships and hovercraft. It explained them at the 'Next Train' exhibition, which was opened by Richard Marsh on the 16th and remained at London's Design Centre until the middle of August.

By this time, Johnson had announced that BR was in the black, but added that he had no illusions about the company's status. Indeed, as *Modern Railways* would note a few months later, while BR had 'the brow of the hill in sight', it was 'not yet over the top'. The trouble was that some of the revenue increase was due not to more freight or passengers being carried, but to 'more effective pricing'. The answer for the former lay perhaps in more block trains, and new wagons; the answer to the latter, BR hoped, was lurking at that exhibition, for there amid the displays of invention and innovation was perhaps the most innovative invention of

Did you know?

Multi-aspect signalling (MAS) increased efficiency, its consistent signal spacing allowing more trains to run on a given line. It also resulted in the closure of many mechanical signal boxes.

BR's Automatic Warning System (AWS) also began to be fitted to more signals on the network throughout the 1960s. The equipment had been designed to alert drivers to 'distant' signals, using magnets in the track and receivers on locomotives. A bell would ring in the cab if the 'distant' was 'off', but a horn would sound if the signal was at 'caution'. This reduced the chance of a train passing a 'stop' signal at danger. An early version had been trialled between King's Cross and Grantham in 1956. By the turn of the decade, it had reached York and would cover almost 3,200 track miles by 1970.

BR's 'Next Train' exhibition of July 1969 featured this futuristic model of the APT.

At around the same time, BR was scoping ideas for the next generation of heavy freight locomotives, which would be capable of exerting 6,000 hp at speeds of up to 125 mph. This model shows how they might have looked had BR continued with the project.

all, in the form of an extraordinary model of a train BR claimed would help make the next decade one 'of progress such as railways have never seen'.

It was understood that anything faster than 125 mph would need a total rethink in terms of track alignment and signalling. The famous Japanese 'bullet trains' were operating at speeds of up to 130 mph on purpose-built lines with gentle gradients and few curves, but the work on 'hunting' undertaken by the ex-aerospace engineers at the Research Division led them to wonder whether faster trains could be run on existing infrastructure by improving rolling stock suspension. From this idea came the Advanced Passenger Train – the APT – which could attain speeds of up to 155 mph, minimising passenger discomfort by tilting into curves. The project had secured partial government funding in 1968 and now had clearance to construct a four-car experimental train, fourteen-mile test track and laboratory.

Also at the exhibition – and much closer to production – was a full-size mock-up of the Mark III carriage, which – like the APT – had come out of the work on 'hunting', but which

the next train...

To accompany the Design Council exhibition, BR produced this brochure, which set out its plans for passenger travel in the 1970s. In addition to the striking APT imagery, it also advertised the company's station, catering, hotel and sleeper service refurbishments, along with its many other facilities.

had become part of the High Speed Diesel Train, an alternative to the APT designed by BR's traditional railway engineers, to whom 125 mph was attainable, and attainable comparatively quickly.

It was fair to say that many of these engineers were decidedly unimpressed with the ex-aerospace 'upstarts', with all their mistakes, re-runs and re-orders, but BR's new Chief Engineer of Traction and Rolling Stock, Terry Miller, could see the potential of the HSDT and submitted a formal proposal to the Board in early 1969. Johnson saw the potential too and gave the project his public support, adding that, if the APT failed to prove itself within the next four to six years, BR would need something reliable to fall back on.

Such was the state of things as 1969 drew to a close. At this stage, no one really knew which train 'the Next Train' would be, so imagine sitting in the Taurus Bar at the rebuilt Birmingham New Street as the autumn gave way to winter. This – BTF told you – was the place to enjoy 'one for the road – the railroad – with impunity'. So you do – a crisp G&T, which you sip from a BR-monogrammed glass before reclining with the *Daily Sketch*. Now imagine being a railway executive doing the same thing, in the same modern surroundings. Perhaps you remember 1960, when steam reigned supreme, and when the pull of the past had been much greater. Not that the past had gone altogether, old signs, old colour schemes, and old ways of doing things living on in odd pockets here and there. Not that the new was without fault or issue, either, there being just as many comparatively new diesels as there were comparatively new steam engines on the scrap lines in 1969, just as there'd been as many bad decisions made as ever there had been and ever there would be.

Yet one seed sown this decade would come to a glorious flowering in the next.

One seed sown. On the sixties railway.

Motorail

More and more motorists are making use of the motorail way to take their cars and families on holiday, without the exhaustion of travelling to and from holiday areas on congested roads. The Motorail network will be developed on selected routes in the 1970s with overnight sleeping accommodation on longer journeys. British Rail pioneered this car-by-train service which is now also operating on continental railways. Motorail users have doubled in the past four years and the service features strongly in the emerging pattern of fast and comfortable passenger travel.

An extract from *Next Train*, detailing plans for BR 'Motorail' car-carrying service, which already allowed motorists to take their vehicles from Swansea to Perth, Stirling to Totnes, Holyhead to Ireland and Newhaven to France.

Above: English Electric Type 4 D212 stands with a brace of Brush 4s at Crewe North stabling point in 1969.
Left: Two gentlemen discuss the future in a First Class compartment. This image is taken from *British Rail is travelling – 1970*, published to herald 'a new era' for the industry.

8
What Now?

Further Reading and Viewing

This book is a summary of British railway history in the 1960s and is not, therefore, an exhaustive survey. More detailed information may be found in the following volumes:

Austin, Chris, and Faulkner, Richard, *Holding the Line: How Britain's Railways Were Saved.* (Oxford Publishing Co., 2012.) *An in-depth study of railway closures, including the Beeching era and its aftermath.*

Bonavia, Michael R., *British Rail: The First 25 Years* (David and Charles, 1981).

Boocock, Colin, *Spotlight on BR: British Railways 1949–1998 – Success or Disaster?* (Atlantic, 1998).

Curtis, Adrian Neil, *Cast of Thousands* (A&C Services, 2001). *A volume packed with archive information about the Western class diesel-hydraulics, including how they came to get their names (as reimagined in Chapter 3).*

Fiennes, G. F., *I Tried to Run a Railway* (Ian Allan, 1967 and 1973). *Includes insights into the introduction of the Deltics, the genesis of BR's 'merry-go-round' coal trains and the problems of constant reorganisation. As noted in Chapter 5, Fiennes' criticism of BR management policy led to his dismissal by Beeching's successor, Stanley Raymond.*

Fiennes, G. F., *Fiennes on Rails* (David & Charles, 1986). *More of the same, from this inspirational railway manager. Includes notes on the Thirsk accident of 1967.*

Gourvish, T. R., *British Railways 1948–73: A Business History* (Cambridge University Press, 1986). *Essential reading for all students of the railway.*

Hardy, R. H. N., *Beeching: Champion of the Railway?* (Ian Allan, 1989). *A more sympathetic view of the Doctor.*

Haresnape, Brian, *British Rail 1948–1978: A Journey by Design* (Ian Allan, 1979). *Covers the design development of locomotives, rolling stock, coach interiors, uniforms, ferries, stations, typefaces and so on.*

Johnson, John, and Long, Robert A., *British Railway Engineering 1948–80* (Mechanical Engineering Publications Ltd, 1981). *The engineering story, told by engineers and verified by those who were actually there.*

Munns, R. T., *Milk Churns to Merry-Go-Round: A Century of Train Operation* (David and Charles, 1986). *A detailed study of the development of freight services. Includes a foreword by Sir Henry Johnson.*

Wolmar, Christian, *Fire and Steam: A New History of the Railways in Britain* (Atlantic Books, 2007). *Sets the 1960s in the wider rail history context.*

The British Film Institute has released a number of British Transport Films' finest documentaries on DVD, including those mentioned in this book, such as *Terminus* and

The Good Way to Travel. They are available from a variety of online and high street stores. Other films available on DVD include:

A Hard Days' Night (1964) – the first Beatles film, which features many on-board scenes. *Black Five* (1968) – commemorates the end of steam in the north-west of England; the DVD includes *The Painter and the Engines* (1967), which details artist David Shepherd's work at Nine Elms during the final months of steam on the Southern.

Web Resources
The National Archives: www.nationalarchives.gov.uk. The National Archives – formerly the Public Record Office – has an online catalogue, listing its collection of official and business-related documents. Copies of some items may be ordered through the site. Visits may also be arranged.

The Railways Archive: www.railwaysarchive.co.uk. Most of the source documents referred to in this book – including the Modernisation Plan and Beeching's two reports – may be downloaded free of charge from this important online resource.

RailServe: www.railserve.com. This is a comprehensive guide to 19,000 railway websites and upcoming events. It features 180 categories, spanning railway travel, railway enthusiasm, and the railway industry.

Search Engine: www.nrm.org.uk/researchandarchive. The National Railway Museum has an extensive online library and archive. Catalogues list details of the museum's extensive collection of papers, drawings, reports, timetables, photographs and so on. Copies of many items can be ordered through the site.

Places to Visit
Museums

Barrow Hill Roundhouse Railway Centre, Campbell Drive, Barrow Hill, Chesterfield, Derbyshire, S43 2PR. Telephone: 01246 472450. Website: www.barrowhill.org.

National Railway Museum, Leeman Road, York, YO26 6XJ. Telephone: 01926 621261. Website: www.nrm.org.uk.

STEAM: Museum of the Great Western Railway, Kemble Drive, Swindon, Wiltshire, SN2 2TA. Telephone: 01793 466646. Website: www.steam-museum.org.uk.

Heritage Railways

Great Central Railway, Loughborough, Leicestershire, LE11 1RW. Telephone: 01509 230726. Website: www.gcrailway.co.uk. *The only double track heritage line in Britain.*

Isle of Wight Steam Railway, The Railway Station, Havenstreet, Isle of Wight, PO33 4DS. Telephone: 01983 882204. Website: www.iwsteamrailway.co.uk. *Experience island rail travel as it was before many lines were closed and Tube trains took over the Ryde–Shanklin route.*